This Gardening Journal Belongs To:

Monthly HARVEST CALENDAR

MONTH:

MONTH:

MONTH:

MONTH:

MONTH:

MONTH:

MONTH:

MONTH:

MONTH:

Gardening Projects

YEARLY GOALS

NEW PROJECTS

TECHNIQUES

NOTES

Produce Budget

FRUIT/VEGETABLE:	WEIGHT/QTY:	PRICE:	MONTHLY:	YEARLY:

Planting Log

PLANT	QTY	START INDOORS	TRANSPLANT	SPACING	HARVEST DATE

Garden Wish List

What fruits or vegetables would you like to grow?

Garden Budget Planner

YEAR:

VEGETABLES	AMOUNT:	FRUIT	AMOUNT:

SUBTOTAL:

FLOWERS	AMOUNT:

SUBTOTAL:

FERTILIZER/MISC	AMOUNT:

SUBTOTAL:

TOTALS	AMOUNT:

SUBTOTAL:

TOTAL:

Seedlings

SEASON: YEAR:

CROP	VARIETY	START	TRANSPLANT	BED/ROW

Weekly To Do

WEEK OF:

TASK	M	T	W	T	F	S	S	NOTES

ADDITIONAL NOTES

Pest Control

BED/ROW	CROP/FAMILY	PEST	DISEASE	TREATMENT:

Sow

SEASON: YEAR:

CROP	VARIETY	SOW/TRANSPLANT	BED/ROW

Seed Inventory

YEAR:

CROP/VARIETY	SEED COMPANY	PURCHASE DATE	QTY

Seed Purchase

YEAR:

CROP/VARIETY	SOURCE	PRICE	QTY

Garden Organizer

YEAR:

BED/ROW	CROPS	SEASON	HARVEST BY	NEXT CROPS

Succession Sowing

YEAR:

CROP	SOW DATE	SEASON	BED/ROW	NOTES

Harvest Tracker

YEAR:

FRUIT/VEG	WEIGHT/QTY	VARIETY	VALUE	NOTES

Crop Rotation

YEAR: _____

BED/ROW	CROP	SEASON	NEXT CROP

Growing

YEAR:

BED/ROW	NOTES (SOIL TEST, ETC)	NOTES

Planner (Sq. Foot)   YEAR:

Seed Packet Info

YEAR:

CROP/ VARIETY	SOWING DEPTH	DAYS TO GERMINATE	DAYS TO MATURITY	HARVEST WINDOW

Gardening Expenses

ITEM#	DESCRIPTION	QTY	PRICE	NOTES

TOTAL EXPENSES

Plant List

CROPS TO GROW
TRACKER

YEAR:

MOST IMPORTANT CROPS

CROPS TO PRESERVE

Fast Growing Crops
READY IN 30-55 DAYS FOR SUCCESSION SOWING

Gardening To Do List

CHORES/ERRANDS: **NOTES:**

Seasonal To Do List

SPRING

SUMMER

FALL

WINTER

Notes

Gardening Notes

Monthly HARVEST CALENDAR

MONTH:

MONTH:

MONTH:

MONTH:

MONTH:

MONTH:

MONTH:

MONTH:

MONTH:

Gardening Projects

YEARLY GOALS

NEW PROJECTS

TECHNIQUES

NOTES

Produce Budget

FRUIT/VEGETABLE:	WEIGHT/QTY:	PRICE:	MONTHLY:	YEARLY:

Planting Log

PLANT	QTY	START INDOORS	TRANSPLANT	SPACING	HARVEST DATE

Garden Wish List

What fruits or vegetables would you like to grow?

Garden Budget Planner

YEAR:

VEGETABLES	AMOUNT:	FRUIT	AMOUNT:

SUBTOTAL:

FLOWERS	AMOUNT:

SUBTOTAL:

FERTILIZER/MISC	AMOUNT:

SUBTOTAL:

TOTALS	AMOUNT:

SUBTOTAL:

TOTAL:

Seedlings

SEASON: YEAR:

CROP	VARIETY	START	TRANSPLANT	BED/ROW

Weekly To Do

WEEK OF:

TASK	M	T	W	T	F	S	S	NOTES

ADDITIONAL NOTES

Pest Control

BED/ROW	CROP/FAMILY	PEST	DISEASE	TREATMENT:

Sow

SEASON: _____ YEAR: _____

CROP	VARIETY	SOW/TRANSPLANT	BED/ROW

Seed Inventory

YEAR:

CROP/VARIETY	SEED COMPANY	PURCHASE DATE	QTY

Seed Purchase

YEAR:

CROP/VARIETY	SOURCE	PRICE	QTY

Garden Organizer

YEAR:

BED/ROW	CROPS	SEASON	HARVEST BY	NEXT CROPS

Succession Sowing

YEAR:

CROP	SOW DATE	SEASON	BED/ROW	NOTES

Harvest Tracker

YEAR:

FRUIT/VEG	WEIGHT/QTY	VARIETY	VALUE	NOTES

Crop Rotation

YEAR:

BED/ROW	CROP	SEASON	NEXT CROP

Growing

YEAR:

BED/ROW	NOTES (SOIL TEST, ETC)	NOTES

Planner (Sq. Foot) YEAR:

Seed Packet Info

YEAR:

CROP/ VARIETY	SOWING DEPTH	DAYS TO GERMINATE	DAYS TO MATURITY	HARVEST WINDOW

Gardening Expenses

ITEM#	DESCRIPTION	QTY	PRICE	NOTES

TOTAL EXPENSES

Plant List

CROPS TO GROW
TRACKER

YEAR:

MOST IMPORTANT CROPS | CROPS TO PRESERVE

Fast Growing Crops
READY IN 30-55 DAYS FOR SUCCESSION SOWING

Gardening To Do List

CHORES/ERRANDS: **NOTES:**

Seasonal To Do List

SPRING

SUMMER

FALL

WINTER

Notes

Gardening Notes

Monthly HARVEST CALENDAR

MONTH:

MONTH:

MONTH:

MONTH:

MONTH:

MONTH:

MONTH:

MONTH:

MONTH:

Gardening Projects

YEARLY GOALS

NEW PROJECTS

TECHNIQUES

NOTES

Produce Budget

FRUIT/VEGETABLE:	WEIGHT/QTY:	PRICE:	MONTHLY:	YEARLY:

Planting Log

PLANT	QTY	START INDOORS	TRANSPLANT	SPACING	HARVEST DATE

Garden Wish List

What fruits or vegetables would you like to grow?

Garden Budget Planner

YEAR:

VEGETABLES	AMOUNT:

SUBTOTAL:

FERTILIZER/MISC	AMOUNT:

SUBTOTAL:

FRUIT	AMOUNT:

SUBTOTAL:

FLOWERS	AMOUNT:

SUBTOTAL:

TOTALS	AMOUNT:

TOTAL:

Seedlings

SEASON: YEAR:

CROP	VARIETY	START	TRANSPLANT	BED/ROW

Weekly To Do

WEEK OF:

TASK	M	T	W	T	F	S	S	NOTES

ADDITIONAL NOTES

Pest Control

BED/ROW	CROP/FAMILY	PEST	DISEASE	TREATMENT:

Sow

SEASON: YEAR:

CROP	VARIETY	SOW/TRANSPLANT	BED/ROW

Seed Inventory

YEAR:

CROP/VARIETY	SEED COMPANY	PURCHASE DATE	QTY

Seed Purchase

YEAR:

CROP/VARIETY	SOURCE	PRICE	QTY

Garden Organizer

YEAR:

BED/ROW	CROPS	SEASON	HARVEST BY	NEXT CROPS

Succession Sowing

YEAR:

CROP	SOW DATE	SEASON	BED/ROW	NOTES

Harvest Tracker

YEAR:

FRUIT/VEG	WEIGHT/QTY	VARIETY	VALUE	NOTES

Crop Rotation

YEAR:

BED/ROW	CROP	SEASON	NEXT CROP

Growing

YEAR:

BED/ROW	NOTES (SOIL TEST, ETC)	NOTES

Planner (Sq. Foot)   YEAR:

Seed Packet Info

YEAR:

CROP/ VARIETY	SOWING DEPTH	DAYS TO GERMINATE	DAYS TO MATURITY	HARVEST WINDOW

Gardening Expenses

ITEM#	DESCRIPTION	QTY	PRICE	NOTES

TOTAL EXPENSES

Plant List

CROPS TO GROW
TRACKER

YEAR:

MOST IMPORTANT CROPS

CROPS TO PRESERVE

Fast Growing Crops
READY IN 30-55 DAYS FOR SUCCESSION SOWING

Gardening To Do List

CHORES/ERRANDS: **NOTES:**

- [ ]
- [ ]
- [ ]
- [ ]
- [ ]
- [ ]
- [ ]
- [ ]
- [ ]
- [ ]
- [ ]
- [ ]
- [ ]
- [ ]
- [ ]
- [ ]

Seasonal To Do List

SPRING **SUMMER**

FALL **WINTER**

Notes

Gardening Notes

Monthly HARVEST CALENDAR

MONTH:

MONTH:

MONTH:

MONTH:

MONTH:

MONTH:

MONTH:

MONTH:

MONTH:

Gardening Projects

YEARLY GOALS

NEW PROJECTS

TECHNIQUES

NOTES

Produce Budget

FRUIT/VEGETABLE:	WEIGHT/QTY:	PRICE:	MONTHLY:	YEARLY:

Planting Log

PLANT	QTY	START INDOORS	TRANSPLANT	SPACING	HARVEST DATE

Garden Wish List

What fruits or vegetables would you like to grow?

Garden Budget Planner

YEAR:

VEGETABLES	AMOUNT:	FRUIT	AMOUNT:

SUBTOTAL:

FLOWERS	AMOUNT:

SUBTOTAL:

FERTILIZER/MISC	AMOUNT:

SUBTOTAL:

TOTALS	AMOUNT:

SUBTOTAL:

TOTAL:

Seedlings

SEASON:　　　　　YEAR:

CROP	VARIETY	START	TRANSPLANT	BED/ROW

Weekly To Do

WEEK OF:

TASK	M	T	W	T	F	S	S	NOTES

ADDITIONAL NOTES

Pest Control

BED/ROW	CROP/FAMILY	PEST	DISEASE	TREATMENT:

Sow

SEASON: YEAR:

CROP	VARIETY	SOW/TRANSPLANT	BED/ROW

Seed Inventory

YEAR:

CROP/VARIETY	SEED COMPANY	PURCHASE DATE	QTY

Seed Purchase

YEAR:

CROP/VARIETY	SOURCE	PRICE	QTY

Garden Organizer

YEAR:

BED/ROW	CROPS	SEASON	HARVEST BY	NEXT CROPS

Succession Sowing

YEAR:

CROP	SOW DATE	SEASON	BED/ROW	NOTES

Harvest Tracker

YEAR:

FRUIT/VEG	WEIGHT/QTY	VARIETY	VALUE	NOTES

Crop Rotation

YEAR:

BED/ROW	CROP	SEASON	NEXT CROP

Growing

YEAR:

BED/ROW	NOTES (SOIL TEST, ETC)	NOTES

Planner (Sq. Foot)   YEAR:

Seed Packet Info

YEAR:

CROP/ VARIETY	SOWING DEPTH	DAYS TO GERMINATE	DAYS TO MATURITY	HARVEST WINDOW

Gardening Expenses

ITEM#	DESCRIPTION	QTY	PRICE	NOTES

TOTAL EXPENSES

Plant List

CROPS TO GROW
TRACKER

YEAR:

MOST IMPORTANT CROPS

CROPS TO PRESERVE

Fast Growing Crops
READY IN 30-55 DAYS FOR SUCCESSION SOWING

Gardening To Do List

CHORES/ERRANDS: **NOTES:**

Seasonal To Do List

SPRING

SUMMER

FALL

WINTER

Notes

Gardening Notes

Monthly HARVEST CALENDAR

MONTH:

MONTH:

MONTH:

MONTH:

MONTH:

MONTH:

MONTH:

MONTH:

MONTH:

Gardening Projects

YEARLY GOALS

NEW PROJECTS

TECHNIQUES

NOTES

Produce Budget

FRUIT/VEGETABLE:	WEIGHT/QTY:	PRICE:	MONTHLY:	YEARLY:

Planting Log

PLANT	QTY	START INDOORS	TRANSPLANT	SPACING	HARVEST DATE

Garden Wish List

What fruits or vegetables would you like to grow?

Garden Budget Planner

YEAR:

VEGETABLES	AMOUNT:	FRUIT	AMOUNT:

SUBTOTAL:

FLOWERS	AMOUNT:

SUBTOTAL:

FERTILIZER/MISC	AMOUNT:

SUBTOTAL:

TOTALS	AMOUNT:

SUBTOTAL:

TOTAL:

Seedlings

SEASON:　　　　　YEAR:

CROP	VARIETY	START	TRANSPLANT	BED/ROW

Weekly To Do

WEEK OF:

TASK	M	T	W	T	F	S	S	NOTES

ADDITIONAL NOTES

Pest Control

BED/ROW	CROP/FAMILY	PEST	DISEASE	TREATMENT:

Sow

SEASON: YEAR:

CROP	VARIETY	SOW/TRANSPLANT	BED/ROW

Seed Inventory

YEAR:

CROP/VARIETY	SEED COMPANY	PURCHASE DATE	QTY

Seed Purchase

YEAR: _____

CROP/VARIETY	SOURCE	PRICE	QTY

Garden Organizer

YEAR:

BED/ROW	CROPS	SEASON	HARVEST BY	NEXT CROPS

Succession Sowing

YEAR: _____

CROP	SOW DATE	SEASON	BED/ROW	NOTES

Harvest Tracker

YEAR:

FRUIT/VEG	WEIGHT/QTY	VARIETY	VALUE	NOTES

Crop Rotation

YEAR:

BED/ROW	CROP	SEASON	NEXT CROP

Growing

YEAR:

BED/ROW	NOTES (SOIL TEST, ETC)	NOTES

Planner (Sq. Foot) YEAR:

Seed Packet Info

YEAR:

CROP/ VARIETY	SOWING DEPTH	DAYS TO GERMINATE	DAYS TO MATURITY	HARVEST WINDOW

Gardening Expenses

ITEM#	DESCRIPTION	QTY	PRICE	NOTES

TOTAL EXPENSES

Plant List

CROPS TO GROW
TRACKER

YEAR:

MOST IMPORTANT CROPS

CROPS TO PRESERVE

Fast Growing Crops
READY IN 30-55 DAYS FOR SUCCESSION SOWING

Gardening To Do List

CHORES/ERRANDS:　　　　　　　　　　　**NOTES:**

Seasonal To Do List

SPRING

SUMMER

FALL

WINTER

Notes

Gardening Notes

Monthly HARVEST CALENDAR

MONTH:

MONTH:

MONTH:

MONTH:

MONTH:

MONTH:

MONTH:

MONTH:

MONTH:

Gardening Projects

YEARLY GOALS

NEW PROJECTS

TECHNIQUES

NOTES

Produce Budget

FRUIT/VEGETABLE:	WEIGHT/QTY:	PRICE:	MONTHLY:	YEARLY:

Planting Log

PLANT	QTY	START INDOORS	TRANSPLANT	SPACING	HARVEST DATE

Garden Wish List

What fruits or vegetables would you like to grow?

Garden Budget Planner

YEAR:

VEGETABLES	AMOUNT:	FRUIT	AMOUNT:

SUBTOTAL:

FLOWERS	AMOUNT:

SUBTOTAL:

FERTILIZER/MISC	AMOUNT:

SUBTOTAL:

TOTALS	AMOUNT:

SUBTOTAL:

TOTAL:

Seedlings

SEASON: _____ YEAR: _____

CROP	VARIETY	START	TRANSPLANT	BED/ROW

Weekly To Do

WEEK OF:

TASK	M	T	W	T	F	S	S	NOTES

ADDITIONAL NOTES

Pest Control

BED/ROW	CROP/FAMILY	PEST	DISEASE	TREATMENT:

Sow

SEASON: YEAR:

CROP	VARIETY	SOW/TRANSPLANT	BED/ROW

Seed Inventory

YEAR:

CROP/VARIETY	SEED COMPANY	PURCHASE DATE	QTY

Seed Purchase

YEAR:

CROP/VARIETY	SOURCE	PRICE	QTY

Garden Organizer

YEAR:

BED/ROW	CROPS	SEASON	HARVEST BY	NEXT CROPS

Succession Sowing

YEAR:

CROP	SOW DATE	SEASON	BED/ROW	NOTES

Harvest Tracker

YEAR:

FRUIT/VEG	WEIGHT/QTY	VARIETY	VALUE	NOTES

Crop Rotation

YEAR:

BED/ROW	CROP	SEASON	NEXT CROP

Growing

YEAR:

BED/ROW	NOTES (SOIL TEST, ETC)	NOTES

Planner (Sq. Foot) YEAR:

Seed Packet Info

YEAR:

CROP/ VARIETY	SOWING DEPTH	DAYS TO GERMINATE	DAYS TO MATURITY	HARVEST WINDOW

Gardening Expenses

ITEM#	DESCRIPTION	QTY	PRICE	NOTES

TOTAL EXPENSES

Plant List

CROPS TO GROW
TRACKER

YEAR:

MOST IMPORTANT CROPS

CROPS TO PRESERVE

Fast Growing Crops
READY IN 30-55 DAYS FOR SUCCESSION SOWING

Gardening To Do List

CHORES/ERRANDS: **NOTES:**

- [ ]
- [ ]
- [ ]
- [ ]
- [ ]
- [ ]
- [ ]
- [ ]
- [ ]
- [ ]
- [ ]
- [ ]
- [ ]
- [ ]
- [ ]
- [ ]

Seasonal To Do List

SPRING

SUMMER

FALL

WINTER

Notes

Gardening Notes

Monthly HARVEST CALENDAR

MONTH:

MONTH:

MONTH:

MONTH:

MONTH:

MONTH:

MONTH:

MONTH:

MONTH:

Gardening Projects

YEARLY GOALS

NEW PROJECTS

TECHNIQUES

NOTES

Produce Budget

FRUIT/VEGETABLE:	WEIGHT/QTY:	PRICE:	MONTHLY:	YEARLY:

Planting Log

PLANT	QTY	START INDOORS	TRANSPLANT	SPACING	HARVEST DATE

Made in the USA
Coppell, TX
16 January 2021